CREAT[E]IVE WRITING

SPARKLING BITS OF WRITING
BOOK 1

WRITING

-JENNIFER YODER

Creative Writing Sparkling Bits of Writing Book I
Copyright © 2019 Jennifer Yoder

Published by Creative Word Studio
Elida, Ohio 45807
creativewordstudio.com
Printed in the United States
ISBN: 978-1-7923-2058-3

CONTRIBUTING ARTISTS:
Eddie Slabaugh
Ariana Miller
Andrew Yoder
Jennifer Yoder

INTRODUCTION . . .

Dear Students,

Welcome to writing class! Writing happens all the time. It happens when you chalk out a pretend story on the sidewalk, journal how you feel, make lists of what to take on vacation, or design a card for Grandma. Swirls, flourishes, and swoops characterize your handwriting and give your letters and lists a personal feel.

I began noticing how people write when I was in sixth grade. I read reports that other people had written and thought, "surely this doesn't have to be so boring! Why does everyone write the same old way?" So I began rethinking how to begin my reports and essays. I wrote stories in my spare time. I poured my heart into every paper I handed into the teacher. Once my teacher wrote back to me in a note, "Jennifer, someday you'll be an author of a book. I hope to read it." I was stunned. Could I be a writer? Although that note went to my head, one positive thing it did was give me the encouragement I needed to pursue writing with a passion. Later that same teacher gave me an editing book to help me along even more. She was the biggest instrument in helping me get several stories published and in pushing me towards writing.

Writing is not confined to stodgy blank pages and reports for science. Writing is observation and creativity. Ask yourself, "How can I word this in a way that is fresh? How can I convey my message in a way that nobody else has before"? It makes you start looking at life through a new lens. When you write creatively, you try to write with interest, pop, and reality. The mundane can become fascinating depending on how we portray it.

Write things down! That is one way to become a good writer. Recording details, conversations, article titles, funny happenings, and things you like or dislike suddenly becomes your "writer's ammunition". You have a wealth of true-to-life tidbits to add to any non-fiction or fiction writing. It's authentic. It's you.

Another way to become a good writer is to observe how others do it. When you read something, notice how you feel about it. Did it bore you and make you toss it aside with a sigh? Or did you reread parts, cling to every word, and formulate a response in your mind? If you did the latter, take note of how that author did it. What style of sentences did he use? What word choices? How can I do that?

Writing doesn't come easily or naturally all the time. But it's something that is worth doing with your whole heart. The more you write, the more comfortable you'll be and success will come quickly. This creative writing course is designed to add some fun and flair to the writing process, divided into small, manageable lessons. I hope you enjoy it! Live with your eyes wide open. Acknowledge the Creator of life. And write with gusto.

Practice makes perfect,

~ Jennifer Yoder

INSTRUCTIONS . . .

There are three basic kinds of lessons in this writing course. Each lesson will be labeled with one of the following kinds of lessons: (1) Free writing, (2) Reading Responses, and (3) Mini Writing Lesson exercises.

Free-writing is a technique used to help you get comfortable with writing whatever you want to. You are expected to write non-stop for a set amount of time (eight minutes or ten minutes, whatever the teacher requires). Write whatever comes to your mind. Normally, the free-writing lessons will have a writing prompt, a picture, a poem, or a question for you to respond to. If however, you'd rather write about a different subject, that is ok too! If you run out of words in your mind, fill in with, "What shall I write next, what shall I write next, what shall I write next," till your creative juices get flowing again. Eventually some other topic will come to your mind!

Reading Response Lessons are to help you analyze other people's writings, and critically think about the given situation. It is good to constantly have wholesome literature in front of us, and this is one way we can do that. Also, we wanted a way for you as students to develop critical thinking skills. One way to do that is to write a response to what you just read. Writing is thinking in this case and it helps summarize your opinions about the writing. We also want you to be able to discern between light and darkness spiritually, especially in reading materials. . ."Is it first pure, then peaceable, of good report. . ." Phil. 4:8?

The Mini Lesson Writing activities are geared toward "fun" writing experiences where you have to "get out of your box" for a bit and try something new! Some lessons might be like what you learn in English Class. All the better! It'll help you know how to make English Class a really good experience for yourself, your classmates, and your teacher. Some of the writing activities are labeled with a symbol ⭐ that stands for a "gold piece". Those are the written pieces that we want you to edit and polish until they're perfected and you are satisfied. It also gives something for the teacher to put a grade on so he/she can record in your report card that you have been doing good writing.

Normally, the lesson plans follow this order: Free writing, Mini Writing Lesson, Reading Response, Mini Writing Lesson, Mini Writing Lesson. . .

Another thing. . .whenever you see this symbol 🤝 it means that it's a friends lesson. You get to pull aside a friend, and do the lesson together! Remember that when you do it with a friend, only help each other think - don't copy each other's work.

TABLE OF CONTENTS . . .

NAME _____   DATE _____

Write an "all about me" acrostic.

Make an acrostic with your first and last name, using phrases to describe yourself by using the beginning letter of your name. If your first name has four or fewer letters, add your middle name. ☺

Read the example, than you try it!

Example:

Talented with inventing things

Happiest when surrounded by chickens

Eats popcorn by the bucketful

Owns a python snake for a pet

Daring swimmer

Opinionated about Paul Bunyan

Red-headed

Eeyore liker

_____

_____

_____

_____

_____

_____

_____

_____

_____

_____

_____

_____

_____

_____

NAME _____   DATE _____

Today, write whatever comes to your mind. Remember that if you get stuck not knowing what to write next, simply pen a few phrases like the following: What shall I write next? What shall I write next? What shall I write next? ☺ Simply start writing phrases, words, exclamations, stories, opinions, or whatever comes to your mind.

Free writing starter question: How do you feel right now? Write at least five phrases that describe how you feel.

Free writing example: I feel "stick-to-my-seat" warm, with an ice cream brain freeze. I feel like Laura Ingalls Wilder when she met Nelly Olson. I feel like I'm rolling on cracker crumbs. I feel happy because I get to run races with my brother Joel tonight…

_____

_____

_____

_____

_____

_____

_____

_____

_____

_____

_____

_____

_____

_____

_____

_____

_____

_____

_____

NAME _____   DATE _____

Write the reasons, or pros and cons for having a smart phone. Here you don't need to worry about grammar and punctuation. You just write. You might have to think a little bit harder because the list has to be a certain length, but that's the fun part of stretching your brain! After all, once your brain is stretched, it'll never return to the original size! ☺ Go ahead, team up with a friend and see what you can come up with.

Write a list of five reasons why everyone should have a smart phone.

_____

_____

_____

_____

_____

Write a list of five reasons why everyone should not have a smart phone.

_____

_____

_____

_____

_____

Now, in the space below, draw a smart phone.

NAME _____   DATE _____

Read:

"…Very soon she heard the soft rustling flight of wings again and she knew at once that the robin had come again. He was very pert and lively, and hopped about so close to her feet, and put his head on one side and looked at her so slyly that she asked Ben Weatherstaff a question.

"Do you think he remembers me?" she said.

"Remembers thee!" said Weatherstaff indignantly. "He knows every cabbage stump in th' gardens, let alone th' people. He's never seen a little wench here before, an' he's bend on findin' out all about thee. Tha's no need to try to hide anything from him."

"Are things stirring down below in the garden where he lives?" Mary inquired.

"What garden?" grunted Weatherstaff, becoming surly again.

"The one where the old rose tress are." She could not help asking, because she wanted so much to know. "Are all the flowers dead, or do some of them come up again in the summer? Are there every any roses?"

"Ask him," said Ben Weatherstaff, hunching his shoulders toward the robin. "He's the only one as knows. No one else has seen inside it for ten year."

Ten years is a long time, Mary thought. She had been born ten years ago.

She walked away, slowly thinking. She had begun to like the garden just as she had begun to like the robin and Dickon and Martha's mother…

. . . .

The robin hopped over a small pile of freshly turned up earth. He stopped on it to look for a worm. The earth had been turned up because a dog had been trying to dig up a mole and he had scratched quite a deep hole. Mary looked at it, not really knowing why the hole was there, and as she looked she saw something almost buried in the newly-turned soil. It was something like a ring of rusty iron or brass, and when the robin flew up into a tree nearby she put out her hand and picked the ring up. It was more than a ring, however; it was an old key which looked as it if had been buried a long time.

Mistress Mary stood up and looked at it with an almost frightened face as it hung from her finger. "Perhaps it has been buried for ten years," she said in a whisper. "Perhaps it is the key to the garden!"

-EXCERPT FROM *THE SECRET GARDEN* BY FRANCES HODGSON BURNETT, CHAPTER 7

Answer the following questions:

1. Who do you think Ben Weatherstaff was?

2. Have you ever talked to a bird or an animal? Write a short dialogue that you could have had with a pet or animal.

3. Why do you think Mary wanted to get inside this garden?

4. What do you think will happen next? Will Mary be able to get inside? Write a paragraph that continues the story.

_____

_____

_____

_____

_____

_____

_____

_____

_____

_____

_____

_____

_____

_____

_____

_____

_____

_____

_____

_____

_____

_____

_____

_____

NAME _____   DATE _____

Today, practice writing strong, concrete nouns to be more specific instead of dull and vague. Here is an example of a dull noun in a sentence: The *flower* shone triumphantly. Here is an example of the same noun replaced with a specific noun: The *Tiger Lily* shone triumphantly.

Strong, concrete nouns give your sentence clearness and spark your audience's interest. Practice replacing vague nouns with concrete nouns.

1. **House:** Example – mansion, igloo, Uncle Tom's Cabin, abode, flat, tepee

2. **Child:** Example – toddler, infant, youngster, pupil, ragamuffin, lass

3. **Bang:** Example – pop, crash _____, _____,

    _____, _____, _____.

4. **Piece of wood:** Example – splinter, log, _____, _____,

    _____, _____, _____.

5. **Bird:** Example – flamingo, _____, _____,

    _____, _____, _____.

6. **Way:** Example – highway, lane, _____, _____,

    _____, _____, _____.

Now, finish out this lesson by writing sentences. ☺

Write a sentence that uses the word "bang" in it. Then dress up the sentence by replacing it with one of your examples. Do the same for the rest of the words. See the difference that using concrete nouns makes?

_____

_____

_____

_____

_____

NAME _____   DATE _____

Today, learn the benefits of using a thesaurus. As you may already know, a thesaurus is a book that has lists of synonyms for the given word. Any writer should use this little book to find the perfect word for his writing. Get used to using a thesaurus almost every time you write. It helps make your writing specific and interesting.

Look up the following words, and add three synonyms to the group of words.

1. Happy, delighted, merry, satisfied

2. Pretty, attractive, handsome, elegant

3. Fast, _____, _____, _____.

4. Head, _____, _____, _____.

5. Grim, _____, _____, _____.

6. Fastidious, _____, _____, _____.

7. Lethargic, _____, _____, _____.

8. Flamboyant, _____, _____, _____.

9. Coax, _____, _____, _____.

10. Apparatus, _____, _____, _____.

When you are finished, pick twelve random words from your list. Assemble them into four groups. Then write a sentence with each group using all three of the words.

Example sentence using synonyms for happy and pretty:

Our merry chorister gave a satisfied smile after we sang an elegant new song.

_____

_____

_____

_____

_____

_____

NAME .... DATE ....

What matters to you?

The souvenir from the Grand Canyon, my collection of rocks, my pocket knife, my Raggedy Ann doll I don't play with anymore, cotton candy, Ronald my pet chicken, a killdeer nest I just found, hearing mom say, "time to get up, its daylight in the swamp!", the memory of dad taking me fishing, mint ice-cream... these all matter to me.

Give yourself a shady circle of lawn and at least five minutes to think before you start writing. Be specific!

_____

_____

_____

_____

_____

_____

_____

_____

_____

_____

To expand the lesson after the free writing is done...

Write why you like five of the things you wrote down.

_____

_____

_____

_____

_____

_____

_____

_____

_____

NAME _____   DATE _____

A well-developed paragraph is a small piece of writing consisting of at least five good sentences. A paragraph includes a topic sentence which states the main idea and is usually at the beginning. The rest of the sentences support, explain, and develop the topic sentence. A summarizing sentence should be at the end of the paragraph to tie all the sentences together.

Example paragraph:

Question: What are the benefits of peanut butter?

Paragraph:

    I think that one of the most important benefits of peanut butter is its excellent taste. A chocolate, peanut butter s'more is one of the best foods in the world because it's creamy, smooth, and slides down your throat into a begging tummy. Peanut butter also gives you energy to go fishing, do chores, or ride bike. It can even calm your nerves before you give a speech in front of your classmates. I definitely think that everyone should like peanut butter!

You try it! Don't forget to start out with a strong topic sentence, and end your paragraph with a summarizing sentence. Use your imagination, add your opinion to the paragraph, create reasons for why you agree or disagree, or write observations on the subject.

Question: Do you think that there are more libraries in the United States, or more McDonald's?

_____

_____

_____

_____

_____

_____

_____

_____

_____

_____

_____

STUDENT TIP:
This is a gold piece lesson. Restudy, edit, and revise your work. Refer to the rubric on the back page on the book for writing tips. Please write the final draft on the following blank page for your teacher to grade.

NAME _____   DATE _____

Read:

The room, in which the boys were fed, was a large stone hall, with a copper at one end: out of which the master, dressed in an apron for the purpose, and assisted by one or two women, ladled the gruel at mealtimes. Of this festive composition each boy had one porringer, and no more—except on occasions of great public rejoicing, when he had two ounces and a quarter of bread besides.

The bowls never wanted washing. The boys polished them with their spoons till they shone again; and when they had performed this operation (which never took very long, the spoons being nearly as large as the bowls), they would sit staring at the copper, with such eager eyes, as if they could have devoured the very bricks of which it was composed; employing themselves, meanwhile, in sucking their fingers most assiduously, with the view of catching up any stray splashes of gruel that might have been cast thereon. Boys have generally excellent appetites. Oliver Twist and his companions suffered the tortures of slow starvation for three months: at last they got so voracious and wild with hunger, that one boy, who was tall for his age, and hadn't been used to that sort of thing (for his father had kept a small cook-shop), hinted darkly to his companions that unless he had another basin of gruel per diem, he was afraid he might some night happen to eat the boy who slept next him, who happened to be a weakly youth of tender age. He had a wild, hungry eye; and they implicitly believed him. A council was held; lots were cast who should walk up to the master after supper that evening, and ask for more; and it fell to Oliver Twist.

The evening arrived; the boys took their places. The master, in his cook's uniform, stationed himself at the copper; his pauper assistants ranged themselves behind him; the gruel was served out; and a long grace was said over the short commons. The gruel disappeared; the boys whispered to each other, and winked at Oliver; while his next neighbors nudged him. Child as he was, he was desperate with hunger, and reckless with misery. He rose from the table; and advancing to the master, basin and spoon in hand, said: somewhat alarmed at his own temerity:

"Please, sire, I want some more."

The master was a fat, healthy man; but he turned very pale. He gazed in stupefied astonishment on the small rebel for some seconds, and then clung for support to the copper. The assistants were paralyzed with wonder; the boys with fear.

"What!" said the master at length, in a faint voice.

"Please, sir," replied Oliver, "I want some more."

The master aimed a blow at Oliver's head with the ladle; pinioned him in his arm; and shrieked aloud for the beadle.

-EXCERPT FROM *OLIVER TWIST* BY CHARLES DICKENS

17

Answer the following questions:

We can only imagine the starvation these boys faced because we've always had plenty to eat.

1. What emotion did you feel toward the following characters as you read?
   The group of boys being served
   The boy that was tall for his age
   Oliver Twist
   The master who hit Oliver

2. Underline ten words that are new or somewhat strange to you and read the definition.

3. Why do you think the boys were not allowed to have any more food.

4. What are three ways the writer helps you see, feel, and hear this scene?

_____

_____

_____

_____

_____

_____

_____

_____

_____

_____

_____

_____

_____

_____

_____

_____

_____

_____

_____

_____

_____

_____

_____

NAME .... DATE ....

I am sure you already know how to write complete sentences. On the other hand, when answering a question, its good practice to make sure we answer correctly so that it is very clear what we are talking about. Always begin your complete answer by restating part of the question first. Try it with the following sentences:

If you could go anywhere on a vacation, where would you go?

Example: If I could go anywhere I wanted to for a vacation I would go to the Australian Outback to photograph kangaroos.

Why is getting ready for church sometimes a long process?

_____

_____

_____

_____

What are two things your dad does when he gets home from work?

_____

_____

_____

_____

If your house was on fire, what three things would you grab?

_____

_____

_____

_____

Would you rather go sky diving or write a book?

_____

_____

_____

_____

How could we make Monday mornings more enjoyable for everyone?

_____

_____

_____

_____

How would you feel if Jesus walked in the door right now?

_____

_____

_____

_____

Who is your favorite author?

_____

_____

_____

_____

_____

_____

_____

_____

_____

_____

_____

_____

_____

NAME _____   DATE _____

Write a description of going swimming without using the following words: Wet, cool, splash, refreshing, water, pool, diving, lake, and swim. Make the description come alive by relating an actual swimming experience. Don't write a "how-to" paragraph.

Here are two examples of written descriptions of eating an ice cream cone without using the following words: ice cream, delicious, vanilla, cone, creamy, cold, lick, bite.

As I walked into Lem's Pizza, my mouth watered with the thought of a white frigid substance that would sooth my dry throat. Once I got my order I dove into it and got a brain freeze.

—SHERLYN YODER (GRADE 8)

I glared at my dog. "There is no way that you are going to get an ittsily bitsily of my chocolatey icily creamily." Nevertheless, in spite of many glares, he sat there patient as ever, hungry as ever, and as cute as ever, waiting for a wee, little itsy, bitsy morsel. At last I gave him a teeny morsel, and then satisfied, he trotted off. I settled back in the hammock. Ahhh…it's almost a shame to eat such a beautifully swirled icily creamily Conifer. I looked at the chocolatey goodness, I couldn't resist. My tingling tongue polished off a wee little bit.

—ARIANA MILLER (GRADE 8)

You try it!

_____
_____
_____
_____
_____
_____
_____
_____
_____
_____
_____
_____
_____
_____

NAME _____   DATE _____

Write an imaginary journal entry by Gideon, Abraham, David, or Jeremiah.

Example journal entry:

Sunday: This morning I watched sheep. Bruno, the brown headed sheep, kept running away. I pulled up a poisonous weed that a sheep was about to eat. Also I played on my harp to keep the sheep calm.

Monday: This morning was quite cool. One of the lambs ran away. I found it over the hill behind a stubby bush. All of a sudden I heard a growl on the far side of the sheep herd. It was a bear. I grabbed my sling shot and began to whirl it. I hit the bear on the head. It crashed to the ground.

Tuesday: This morning not much happened. I found a snake near a lamb in the afternoon. I grabbed my knife and ended its life.

Wednesday: I'm so excited! My father said I'm to take food to my brothers in the army. So I came here today. I got here at bedtime. I get to sleep in my brother's tent. I hope to see a Philistine tomorrow.

Thursday: I got to see a giant today. His name is Goliath. He called me names. I knew I could kill him because God is with me. I used a stone and my slingshot-hurling the stone straight at his forehead. He died, so I cut off his head. My heart beat so hard; I was scared. The Israelites rejoiced over me and what God did.

-DESTANY CARTER (GRADE 6)

_____

_____

_____

_____

_____

_____

_____

_____

_____

_____

_____

NAME _____   DATE _____

Aunt Jolene: "The moon is full tonight. Isn't it pretty?"

Betsie, age 5: "Is it full of milk?"

Joanna, age 4: "No, it's full of cottage cheese!"

Make lists of what the following items might be full of, real or imagined. Be creative!

Examples:

Clover heads: bees searching for nectar, chlorophyl, deer food

Mom's snack cupboard: red guilty faces, graham crackers, cheese curls, sticky fingers

Riverbed _____

Kindergartner's backpack _____

Sixteen-year-old's bedroom _____

An attic _____

A squirrel hole _____

An abandoned shoe _____

A bell tower _____

A little boy's pocket _____

Potato bin _____

A pyramid in Giza of Egypt _____

_____

_____

_____

_____

_____

_____

A KINDERGARTNER'S
BACKPACK

_____

_____

_____

NAME _____   DATE _____

Read:

Have You Ever Seen?

Have you ever seen a sheet on a river bed?

Or a single hair from a hammer's head?

Has the foot of a mountain any toes?

And is there a pair of garden hose?

Does the needle ever wink its eye?

Why doesn't the wing of a building fly?

Can you tickle the ribs of a parasol?

Or open the trunk of a tree at all?

Are the teeth of a rake ever going to bite?

Have the hands of the clock any left or right?

Can the garden plot be deep and dark?

And what is the sound of the birches bark?

-ANONYMOUS

Answer the following questions:

1. Which word picture was your favorite?

2. Explain what a "pun" is.

3. Write three more puns.

Examples: Broken pencils are pointless.
           We deposited the canoe in the riverbank.

_____

_____

_____

NAME _____   DATE _____

It is nearing Thanksgiving! Draw a pumpkin the size of a bowl on this page. Then, fill the pumpkin up with thirty to fifty autumn or thanksgiving words. Think of words like crimson, corncobs, pilgrims, harvest, gold, burnt leaves, etc. The list is nearly endless! ☺

Example:

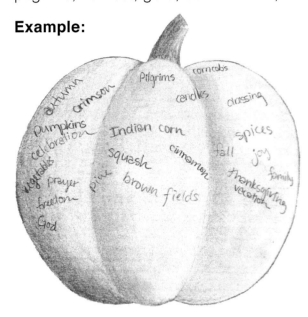

NAME _____   DATE _____

What would you find in an old chest from Grandpa's attic? An old sling shot. Yellowed papers. Lacy bonnet. An envelope of money. A wooden bat. Boots with twenty-five buttons. An old smell. Tennis racket. Pictures of ancestors. A string of beads.

What would you find in your dad's desk? Nubbins of eraser. Hanging files bulging with papers. Bible Study helps. Chocolate Whoppers. Graph paper. House plans. CD's. Envelopes. A list of wonderful things about my mom. A golf ball. Dust bunnies. Prayer cards from church. Dad's checkbook. Calendar. Hordes of paper.

Write ten things you would find in . . .

Your Mom's kitchen

1. _____
2. _____
3. _____
4. _____
5. _____
6. _____
7. _____
8. _____
9. _____
10. _____

Cabela's

1. _____
2. _____
3. _____
4. _____
5. _____
6. _____
7. _____
8. _____
9. _____
10. _____

The town square

1. _____
2. _____
3. _____
4. _____
5. _____
6. _____
7. _____
8. _____
9. _____
10. _____

Big Ben (Look up in encyclopedia.)

1. _____
2. _____
3. _____
4. _____
5. _____
6. _____
7. _____
8. _____
9. _____
10. _____

An African Hut

1. _____
2. _____
3. _____
4. _____
5. _____
6. _____
7. _____
8. _____
9. _____
10. _____

A little boy's pocket

1. _____
2. _____
3. _____
4. _____
5. _____
6. _____
7. _____
8. _____
9. _____
10. _____

_____
_____
_____
_____
_____
_____
_____
_____
_____
_____
_____
_____
_____
_____
_____
_____
_____
_____
_____
_____
_____

NAME _____   DATE _____

The following paragraph is the imaginary thoughts of a school child as he was doing his morning chores.

I'm going to check the barn swallow nest after I'm done here to see if the eggs hatched. Where is the rooster? I sure don't want to be chased this morning. Why does Javon always laugh at me about that rooster chasing me? He says I'm chicken. But I'm not. Oh! What did Delroy find? Another mouse. Dad says Delroy is better than a mousetrap. What will happen today at school? Will Miss Amy make us boys write dictionary pages for careless work again? I hear mom calling – maybe she made crumb cake to eat with our oatmeal. I better hurry!

What do you think about when you are doing your chores?

_____

_____

_____

_____

_____

_____

_____

_____

_____

_____

_____

_____

_____

_____

_____

_____

_____

_____

NAME _____   DATE _____

Wake up your senses! Today you're going to pen another style of poetry.

Examples:

Joy is bright green.

It tastes like orange juice.

It smells like sunshine.

It looks like fireworks.

It sounds like a crackling fire.

Joy makes me feel like giggling.

Crankiness is orange brown.

It tastes like dried out cookies.

It smells like bad breath.

It looks like a bull dog.

It sounds like a chalkboard scratch.

Crankiness is how I feel with a sore throat.

Excitement is _____

It tastes like _____

It smells like _____

It looks like _____

It sounds like _____

Excitement makes me feel _____

Loneliness is _____

It tastes like _____

It smells like _____

It looks like _____

It sounds like _____

Loneliness makes me feel _____

STUDENT TIP:
This is a gold piece lesson. Restudy, edit, and revise your work. Refer to the rubric on the back page on the book for writing tips. Please
write the final draft on the following blank page for your teacher to grade.

NAME _____   DATE _____

Read:

This narrative shows an incident of Tom, whose aunt thinks he is ill. Instead of taking the bad-tasting medicine she insisted upon, he pours it into a crack in the floor. What happens next?

> One day Tom was in the act of dosing the crack when his aunt's yellow cat came along, purring, eyeing the teaspoon avariciously, and begging for a taste. Tom said:
>
> "Don't ask for it unless you want it Peter."
>
> But Peter signified that he did want it.
>
> "You'd better make sure."
>
> Peter was sure.
>
> "Now you've asked for it, and I'll give it to you, because there ain't anything mean about me; but if you find you don't like it, you mustn't blame anybody but your own self."
>
> Peter was agreeable. So Tom pried his mouth open and poured down the Pain-killer. Peter sprang a couple of yards in the air, and then delivered a war-whoop and set off round and round the room, banging against furniture, upsetting flower pots, and making general havoc. Next he rose on his hind feet and pranced around, in a frenzy of enjoyment, with his head over his shoulder and his voice proclaiming his unappeasable happiness. Then he went tearing around the house again spreading chaos and destruction in his path. Aunt Polly entered in time to see him throw a few double somersaults, deliver a final mighty hurrah, and sail through the open window, carrying the rest of the flower-pots with him. The old lady stood petrified with astonishment, peering over her glasses; Tom lay on the floor expiring with laughter.
>
> -EXCERPT FROM *TOM SAWYER*

Answer the following questions:

1. Tom and the cat Peter seem to be having a dialogue. What makes you believe that the cat is answering Tom?

2. Make a list of words that makes the action seem rapid.

3. Make a list of specific words that implies noise and destruction.

4. What do you think happens to Tom next?

5. What will Aunt Polly say?

NAME _____   DATE _____

In writing sentences and paragraphs, you should write with clear, specific words to "show" your reader the mental pictures instead of "telling" them.

One way to accomplish "showing" instead of "telling" is to use active verbs instead of passive verbs like was and were. Practice using strong, active verbs in the following exercises. Think of how you personally would feel in these situations to help make the sentences authentic.

Examples:

Telling sentence: There was a train going up the mountain.
Showing sentence: Hooting and belching, the sooty steam engine chugged up the craggy mountain.

Telling sentence: Randy was nervous while driving.
Showing sentence: Gripping his steering wheel until his knuckles were white, Randy glanced in his mirror.

Telling sentence: I was really scared.
Showing sentence: My heart thudded and I could feel goosebumps race up my arm.

1. It was a hot day.

_____

_____

2. Craig was humiliated.

_____

_____

3. I was so bored.

_____

_____

4. We had terribly much fun!

_____

_____

5. My chicken chores were easy.

NAME _____   DATE _____

Imagine what two nonliving objects might say to each other. Read the following example:

"Hey Walmart, did you ever see this young girl? She has brown hair. Oh, never mind. I found a picture. She comes here every weekend to eat my famous soft pretzels and then does some shopping," said the mall.

"Yes, she comes every four weeks to shop here, but I should talk to her and tell her that Walmart is the best!" replied Walmart.

"No! She likes me better, because our stuff lasts longer than your merchandise. And my mall is bigger than your store Walmart!" retorted the mall.

"Ok! Stop! You're right, but let's just see what happens!" said Walmart.

"Hmmm," mused the brown haired girl, "Looks like I need to go to Walmart, then stop at the mall. Hey! I think I'll do this every time I go to Walmart."

"See," said Walmart, "the girl is coming regularly to Walmart, and to the mall as well. So we are equal now," Walmart exclaimed to the mall.

"Yes!" replied the mall, looking at Walmart. They smiled.

-SHERLYN YODER (GRADE 7)

Today, write an imaginary, mini conversation that could happen between two inanimate objects. Use one of the options below, or think of your own.

-a bike and a four wheeler

-a pet orange and a pet banana

-a hamburger and a hot dog

-a piano and a violin

-a strawberry and a blueberry

-a vacuum cleaner and a wastebasket

-a clothespin and a garden rake

-a fishing pole and a boat anchor

-an old book and a rocking horse

-an apron and a rolling pin

NAME _____   DATE _____

Sometimes there are things that we think we couldn't do without or at least wouldn't want to try. Like certain people, events, seasons, songs, books, colors, dreams, sports, places, scenes, sounds, smells, animals, flowers, feelings, parties, habits, rituals, comforts, etc.

I couldn't do without… (Be specific)

Sample List:

Sunsets behind our barn

Cranberry scones with Devonshire cream

Lilacs blooming

My dog

Anna, my best friend

Dutch Blitz

Winnie the Pooh

Sour Patch Kids

Soccer

My polka dotted mud boots

Snail mail

Mom & Dad

My bike

The Penderwicks

Cold Mint tea

Tomato sandwiches

My lego set

Hallelujah Chorus

Sunday evenings at home

_____

_____

_____

_____

_____

_____

_____

_____

_____

_____

_____

_____

_____

_____

NAME _____   DATE _____

This lesson provides another opportunity to practice the "show instead of tell" technique that good writing needs. The "show instead of tell" technique simply means that you should use strong, specific words. You've already practiced with this by using a thesaurus. Brainstorm with a friend and broaden your vocabulary. Write as many specific words or phrases as you can to replace each example.

1. Walked slowly

_____

_____

_____

_____

2. Eat

_____

_____

_____

_____

3. Get away from

_____

_____

_____

_____

4. Go

_____

_____

_____

_____

5. Looked

_____

_____

_____

_____

NAME _____   DATE _____

Read:

The man-eater crouched for the spring, the tuft of its tail motionless as it flexed its muscles. Almost instantly Ndama's arrow whistled through the air. The shaft struck the man-eater with a smack on the hind quarters.

The animal whirled around, glared savagely for a moment and charged.

Ndama dropped his bow and arrows and ran, shouting to Ochella, "Climb a tree! Climb a tree!"

The man-eater was just behind him when he got to the tree. And now to his horror he discovered that it was a thorn tree. But what did the thorns matter now? He grabbed the nearest limb, thorns and all, and pulled himself up. The lion made a spring, but the spring was short. Ndama climbed as high as he could and then looked over in Ochella's direction. He was safe! His only regret was that the arrow sticking in the lion had not been painted with poison.

Simba, his eyes ablaze with the fury of the Suk plains, growled and leaped at him again. But Ndama was too high

. . . .

"How are we going to get back to the village?" shouted Ochella as the lion looked up at him hungrily.

"I don't know," replied Ndama solemnly. "Maybe we'll have to live here!"

"Well, you ought to know," grumbled Ochella. "You're the one that got us into this mess."

"Father didn't want us to come," continued Ochella, his voice getting louder and higher. "Why do you always try and get us into a mess? Aren't you ever satisfied?"

Ndama refused to talk and Ochella went on bitterly, "We were happy at home, everything was going along fine, our stomachs full of flying ants. Then you got the wonderful idea that we should follow Bwana Greeni into the Suk. If that lion eats us I hope he eats you first. I'll enjoy watching you slide down his throat. All this trouble is your fault. Adventure! Stories to tell! Missionaries! Phup! If we ever get out of this mess I'll never follow any more of your schemes. Never! Never! Never!"

Answer the following questions:

1. Where does this story take place?

2. Would you have responded as Ndama or Ochella?

3. What other animals are "man-eaters"?

4. How would you have felt with a lion coming after you?

5. How do you think these boys got help?

NAME _____   DATE _____

One of the skills that adds pop and flair to a creative writing piece is the use of onomatopoeic ("On-uh-mat-uh-pee-ic") words. Onomatopoeia is when the word sounds like what it names such as the following: hiss, cuckoo, sizzle, plop, etc.

Although the following exercise uses some imagination, think about the sound associated with the word picture. Create a new word for some of these sounds!

Examples:

What is the sound of falling snow? fif-faf-fif-faf

What is the sound of a clothes dryer? bull-in-the-parlor, washin-cleanin-dryin, goats-in-their-pajamas[1]

What is the sound of someone eating popcorn? homf-vach-vach-vach

What is the sound of a siren? woo-wOO-WOO-Woo-woo-wOO-WOO-Woo

1. What is the sound of horses galloping?_____

2. What is the sound of a fawn calling for its mother?_____

3. What is the sound of diligent students?_____

4. What is the sound of fog lifting?_____

5. What is the sound of a tree frog?_____

6. What is the sound of sledding down a hill?_____

7. What is the sound of a chickadee?_____

8. What is the sound of cutting paper? _____

9. What is the sound of rain?_____

10. What is the sound of a circular saw?_____

11. What is the sound of happy people?_____

12. What is the sound of a wood pecker? _____

13. What is the sound of a garden tiller?_____

14. What is the sound of a four-wheeler? _____

15. What is the sound of a church bell?_____

16. What is the sound of a bad attitude? _____

_____

1 From *Summer of Light* by W. Dale Cramer

NAME _____   DATE _____

Write a list of as many colors as you can think of or find. You may look in an encyclopedia, a children's book, or in a crayon box for ideas. You can invent your own colors. See who can write down the most colors.

Example:

Lavender, turquoise, maroon, pink, slate, beige, brown, bronze, melon, lime, rust, salmon. . . .

_____

_____

_____

_____

_____

_____

After you've made your list of colors, use alliteration to expand the colors into amazing word combos. Like this. . .

Example:

Lulling lavender, thundering turquoise, subtle slate, smoldering salmon, majestic melon, blundering beige, bucking bronze, morose maroon, rocking rust, leaping lime, popping purple, tiptoe tan, blasting blue. . .

Doesn't that add amazing flair to the colors? You try it! ☺

_____

_____

_____

_____

_____

_____

_____

_____

_____

NAME _____   DATE _____

Its Christmas time! Start out your free writing today by writing words that are associated with Christmas.

1. _____
2. _____
3. _____
4. _____
5. _____
6. _____
7. _____
8. _____
9. _____
10. _____
11. _____
12. _____
13. _____
14. _____
15. _____
16. _____
17. _____
18. _____
19. _____
20. _____

Now write down several memories you have of Christmas with your family.

_____

_____

_____

_____

_____

_____

NAME _____   DATE _____

Brainstorm with a friend all the different ways we use the word "down" in phrases, sayings, words, expressions etc. For example, we use the word "down" in downstairs, down under, thumbs down, go down, slow down, weigh down, write down, download, feeling down, two down-three to go, and many other ways. Think of ten or more phrases or words. If your teacher has one, check out a rhyming dictionary for ideas on this one!

_____

_____

_____

_____

_____

_____

Then compile your phrases into a short paragraph story using all the phrases or words.

Here is an example of a paragraph story using the word "set" repetitiously. ☺

It becomes a backset when we have a mindset that we can only use set. We were beset because our asset, a tea set, was offset. And so we became upset, because our asset was offset. We had to reset the rosette on our heavy set dresser set. While we set the table and set the chairs we saw a beautiful sunset and moonset. Even though we are thick set and heavy set we are well set for upsetting the fruit basket. And thanks for not being upset about our mindset that we can only use the word set.

- BY ARIANA MILLER AND TIFFANY RABATIN (GRADE 8)

_____

_____

_____

_____

_____

_____

_____

_____

_____

NAME _____   DATE _____

Read:

"A Little Bird I Am"
LOUISA MAY ALCOTT

A little bird I am,
Shut from the fields of air,
And in my cage I sit and sing
To Him who placed me there:
Well pleased a prisoner to be,
Because, my God, it pleases Thee!

'Naught have I else to do;
I sing the whole day long;
And He whom most I love to please
Doth listen to my song,
He caught and bound my wandering wing,
But still He bends to hear me sing.

Answer the following questions:

1. When do you feel like a caged bird?

2. What does line five mean?

3. Summarize the theme of the poem.

4. Write three times you feel like a caged bird.

5. Write three things that are opposite of a caged bird.

_____

_____

_____

NAME _____   DATE _____

It's amazing what one word makes you think of. Mental pictures, smells, and feelings come to our minds instantly when we hear or read words. Write the first thing that comes to your mind when you read the top word.

Then put a little arrow below it. After that, write the next word that comes to your mind. Notice the example below:

Marshmallow   Jay-walked   Dream   Moses   Crimson   Flicker
↓
Campfire
↓
Lightning bugs
↓
Dewy grass
↓
Grass stuck to feet
↓
Bedtime
↓
Sleep
↓
Groggy wake up time
↓
Tired eyes
↓
Breakfast
↓
Eggs
↓
Family devotions
↓
Singing
↓
Dishes
↓
Brush teeth
↓
Peppermint
↓
Clean

NAME _____   DATE _____

Get together with your class. Each of you should write ten nouns, ten verbs, and ten adjectives on slips of paper. Put them into the "Word Deposit Box". Draw ten words. Write a paragraph, a short story, or a one stanza poem using all your words. The writings should include a specific theme.

Examples:

The ten words: soup, winter, heart, lumber, mink, greed, barren, splashing, dream, swiftly

The short story:

One evening in early **winter**, a wood cutter sat at his table counting his money. His **soup** sat untouched beside him, **swiftly** growing cold. As he imagined what his day would be like tomorrow, he fell asleep. While he was sleeping, he had a **dream**. He dreamed that there was once a man with a **heart** like stone. To make money, he cut down trees in the forest for **lumber**. As he cut them down, his **greed** grew. He heartlessly started killing every animal that got in his way. **Mink**, raccoon, hawks, eagles, and rabbits were killed and thrown aside to be decomposed. Soon, no animals were left, and the **barren** land was still and quiet. Too quiet. The man built himself a mansion, and had enough money to live comfortably for the rest of his life. But with no trees there, the wind howled listlessly, and the man soon grew lonely. He went to town and bought trees of every kind. He planted them all around his house. He tenderly cared for them and soon the trees grew tall and strong. But the happy chatter of birds and the sounds of **splashing** water could not be heard again and...the woodcutter awoke with a start. That had been himself he was dreaming about. "I will leave the woods as they are," he vowed to himself, "and not let my greed destroy nature!" And he did.

-JULIEANNA YODER (GRADE 8)

The ten words: gigantic, bandit, old-fashioned, toothpick, love, advertise, sunrise, preposterous, icicles, world

The short story:

Once there was a **gigantic** bellied **bandit** who sold **old-fashioned toothpicks**. He **loved** to **advertise** them. Then on Monday morning at **sunrise**, something **preposterous** happened. His toothpicks were gone! But wait, there were **icicles** all over the **world**. Even on his nose.

- JADON GINGERICH (GRADE 6)

_____

_____

_____

_____

STUDENT TIP:
This is a gold piece lesson. Restudy, edit, and revise your work. Refer to the rubric on the back page on the book for writing tips. Please write the final draft on the following blank page for your teacher to grade.

NAME _____   DATE _____

Which part of speech are you?

Noun: the center of attention; person in charge; popular

Action Verb: always doing something

Being Verb: always helping; pointing to others

Pronoun: does things for other people

Adjective: helps others be valuable

Adverb: helps verb people get their stuff done

Conjunction: makes connections between people; connects ideas

Preposition: makes outsiders feel included; friendly

Interjection: the drama queen

Think about which part of speech you are the most like. Write about why you feel you might be a verb, or adjective, or interjection. ☺

Example:

    Most days I feel like an adverb. I feel like I am always helping my mom do dishes or sweep the floor. I like being an adverb with mom when she is baking cookies. I really like being an adverb with dad because everything he does is fun! Sometimes he is even an adverb to us and helps us do the chores. I probably should be an adverb more often to my siblings than I do. I should start helping them do chores even when it is not my turn.

-AARON MILLER (GRADE 6)

_____

_____

_____

_____

_____

_____

_____

NAME _____   DATE _____

Today you are going to write a mini poem called a diamante (dee-ah-mahn-tay). A diamante is a seven line contrasting poem which is set up in the shape of a diamond.

Line 1. Write one word (a noun, the subject)

Line 2. Write two adjectives describing the noun

Line 3. Write three words that end in "ing" that are associated with the original word.

Line 4. Write four words (first two should relate to line 1, the last two words should relate to line 7)

Line 5. Write three words (that end in "ing" or "ed" relating to line 7)

Line 6. Write two adjectives describing the noun.

Line 7. Write one word (opposite or contrasting to line 1)

(Hint - it is easiest to start with lines 1 and 7 first)

Here are some ideas:

1. Child/Adult
2. Smile/Frown
3. Student/Teacher
4. River/Ocean
5. Day/Night
6. Jungle/Desert

Example:

Black

Mysterious, midnight

Darkening, frightening, defiling

Dirtied, smudged, bleached, cleaned,

Purifying, brightening, dazzling

Snowy, pure

White

STUDENT TIP:
This is a gold piece lesson. Restudy, edit, and revise your work. Refer to the rubric on the back page on the book for writing tips. Please write the final draft on the following blank page for your teacher to grade.

65

NAME _____ DATE _____

Read:

Snow

I like whirling, white snow,
Bright snow,
Slight snow,
Certain-to-excite snow,
Falling through the night.
Scoop-with-all-your-might snow,
Fluffy-fuzz-in-flight snow
Heaping-any-height-snow,
Landing soft and light.

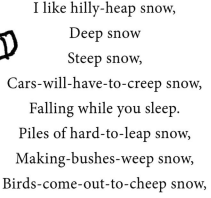

I like hilly-heap snow,
Deep snow
Steep snow,
Cars-will-have-to-creep snow,
Falling while you sleep.
Piles of hard-to-leap snow,
Making-bushes-weep snow,
Birds-come-out-to-cheep snow,
Fleecy as a sheep

I like lots of late snow,
Great snow
Straight now,
Sled and sleigh and skate snow,
Shout and celebrate.
We-can-hardly-wait snow,
Falling-five-to-eight snow,
Who could ever hate snow?
Snow is always great!

-LUCY A. MARTIN

Answer the following questions:

1. What do you like about snow?

2. What do you like about this poem?

3. Have you seen all these different kinds of snow?

4. Write down two things you like to do in the snow.

_____

_____

_____

_____

_____

_____

_____

_____

_____

_____

_____

_____

_____

_____

_____

_____

_____

_____

_____

_____

_____

_____

_____

NAME _____ DATE _____

Today, write a sales pitch for something in your classroom or gym. Persuade your reader to switch to your product that you are "selling".

Examples:

I think Elmer's glue is the kind of glue to use. It's transportable and it's the kind for children because it's non-toxic! It lasts longer than other glue and is in liquid form. Not to mention, it's very handy. If I was going to buy glue, I would pick Elmer's glue. Best of all, you can find it at most any store.

-NAOMI RABATIN (GRADE 6)

Thank-you for your interest in White Erasers. Currently they are the most used and appreciated in Zion Christian School by both students and teachers. They erase marks 75% better than other erasers. The eraser remains flexible and white in spite of heavy use. What boy would like a pink eraser anyway? Realistically, this eraser is simply top-of-the-line! Although there are many other erasers out there to buy, you're going to want to buy one of these white erasers. The good thing about white erasers? You can buy them at Walmart! Better prices, better color, better results! Who can resist? ☺

_____

_____

_____

_____

_____

_____

_____

_____

_____

_____

_____

_____

_____

_____

_____

_____

NAME _____   DATE _____

Today, we will write the simple paragraph again. An excellent paragraph is developed in three main ways. You can show good development by giving examples, telling incidents, or by giving reasons to support your topic sentence.

Write a paragraph answering one of the following questions:

1. *Should children get money allowances every month?*
   Use good examples to prove your point.

2. *Why should you keep your distance from bears in the wild?*
   Use incidents to illustrate the point.

3. *Why should we go to bed early?*
   Use valid reasons to support your ideas.

_____

_____

_____

_____

_____

_____

_____

_____

_____

_____

_____

_____

_____

_____

_____

_____

_____

_____

STUDENT TIP:
This is a gold piece lesson. Restudy, edit, and revise your work. Refer to the rubric on the back page on the book for writing tips. Please write the final draft on the following blank page for your teacher to grade.

NAME _____   DATE _____

In eight minutes list many places you could go. Here are some to get you started.........Asia, laundry room, Burger King, Tyler's house, Super Eight, Dick's Sporting Goods, mower shed, library, forest, JCPenny's, science class, Montana, church, principal's office......

_____

_____

_____

_____

_____

_____

_____

_____

_____

_____

_____

_____

_____

_____

_____

_____

_____

_____

_____

_____

_____

_____

_____

NAME _____   DATE _____

Write a list of words or phrases that widen your understanding of a circle. Name everything that you imagine tastes, feels, or looks round to you. Draw several circles as doodle art and imagine what they could be.

Example list:

Oreo's

Outer rim of a tea cup

A Hula-Hoop

Sunglasses

Speck of oatmeal on your chin

A polka dot

Bubble

Path around the school house

A singer's mouth

A peep hole

NAME _____   DATE _____

Read:

After his meeting with the bishop he often wandered up into the neighborhood of St. Mark's with a vague hope that he might see again the man who seemed to his boyish imagination a very king among men. It had long been Tode's secret ambition to grow into a big, strong man himself-bigger and stronger than the common run of men. Now, whenever he thought about it, he said to himself, "Just like the bishop."

But he never met the bishop, and having found out that he did not preach regularly at St. Mark's, Tode never went there after the second time.

One afternoon in late September, the boy was lounging along with Tag at his heels in the neighborhood of the church, when he heard a great rattling of wheels and clattering of hoofs, and around the corner came a pair of horses dragging a carriage that swung wildly from side to side, as the horses came tearing down the street. There was no one in the carriage, but the driver was puffing along a little way behind, yelling frantically, "Stop 'em! Stop em! Why don't ye stop the brutes!"

There were not many people on the street and the few men within sight seemed not at all anxious to risk life or limb in an attempt to stop horses going at such a reckless pace.

Now Tode was only a little fellow not yet fourteen, but he was strong and lithe as a young Indian, and as to fear-he did not know what it was. As he saw the horses dashing toward him he leaped into the middle of the street and stood there, eyes alert and limbs ready, directly in their pathway. They swerved aside as they approached him, but with a quick upward spring he grabbed the bit of the one nearest him and hung there with all his weight. This frightened and maddened the horse, and he plunged and reared and flung his head from side to side, until he succeeded in throwing the boy off. The delay however, slight as it was, had given the driver time to come up, and he speedily regained control of his team while a crowd quickly gathered.

Tode had been flung off sidewise, his head striking the curbstone, and there he lay motionless......

-EXCERPT FROM *THE BISHOP'S SHADOW* BY I.T.THURSTON
©COPYRIGHT PERMISSION GRANTED OCT. 23, 2017

Answer the following questions:

1. Tell us what you think the bishop was like.

2. The bishop obviously was Tode's hero. Who is someone you respect and why?

3. It says in the story that Tode didn't know what fear was. Why not?

4. What do you think happened next?

_____

_____

_____

_____

_____

_____

_____

_____

_____

_____

_____

_____

_____

_____

_____

_____

_____

_____

_____

_____

_____

_____

_____

NAME _____   DATE _____

Today you are going to ease into some easy poetry. ☺ Read the examples below.

Examples:

Who: The tawny lion

What: yawned ominously

When: after his lunch

Where: under the shade tree

Why: ready for his nap in the heat.

Who: Our professor

What: always clicks his pencil

When: while it's quiet

Where: during study hall

Why: because he doesn't have anything else to do.

You try it!

Who: _____

What: _____

When: _____

Where: _____

Why: _____

Who: _____

What: _____

When: _____

Where: _____

Why: _____

NAME _____   DATE _____

A weather gram is a brief sentence or sudden inspiration of ten words or less having to do with nature. It is written on a brown paper bag, book mark style, and should be hung outside to "weather" for three months. It can be hung along a woodsy trail, in the garden, on a tree branch, at a campsite, on a barn, or wherever! Design one in the space given below, and then transfer to a brown paper bag. Ask permission from your teacher or parents to hang yours outside to "weather".

Examples:

Sparkling dewdrops display glass globes of color.

Whispering pines tell you the way back home.

If you carry flowers butterflies may follow your footsteps.

_____

_____

_____

_____

_____

_____

_____

_____

_____

_____

_____

_____

_____

_____

_____

_____

_____

_____

_____

NAME _____   DATE _____

I am sure you have written a letter before. But suppose you wrote a letter every single Monday morning to the same person, what would you tell them? ☺ They would know all your family's names. They would know all the activities you have been doing at school and at home lately. They would know a lot of things! But I'm sure that person would LOVE hearing from you week after week after week. Who would that person be?

Your Grandma?

Your hero?

Your married sibling?

Your cousin?

The President?

The janitor at church?

The electric company?

The greeter at Walmart?

Pooh Bear?

Sherlock Holmes?

The clerk at Dairy Queen?

Example (a true happening):

Dear Sherlock Holmes,

　　Hello! We 8th grade girls at Zion Christian School are wondering if you would come help us solve a mysterious case. One afternoon in April we discovered a mysterious ramshackle house. Of course we decided to explore it. However as soon as we stepped into the door way we knew something was strange about the house. A piano that still works? A floor littered with shoes, purses, brooms, etc.? A stuffed lamb on the heater? Dishes in the drainer? And a baking mitt on the stove? What is this all about? However, that is not as bad compared to what we saw next. On the door leading to the basement we saw blood. Someone had written their initial T.A.M. on the door. Can you help us solve the mystery?

Love, Ariana and friends

NAME _____   DATE _____

When you are writing a paragraph, you should write coherently. Coherence means that you arrange details in an easy-to-understand type of way. It makes your audience better able to understand your paragraph. There is chronological order - time, when it happened. There is spatial order - either near to far, top to bottom, left to right. There is order of importance.

Using the following list of transitional words helps make your writing flow smoothly from one detail to the next:
Again, also, and, but, yet, nor, first, second, third, finally, in addition, next, beyond, here, in the distance, opposite to, to the left, to the right, then, therefore, above, across from, before me, below me, for instance, etc.

Write a paragraph about the place you go to when you want to be alone. Is it in the haymow? The woods behind the house? Your bedroom? Dad's study? Up on the hill? Describe it in detail, showing us the place with word pictures.

Example:

One of the most wonderful places to be alone is my dear violet patch, one of the most precious gold mines I have chanced to discover. 'Tis the dearest little patch of violets in the whole world, forming a wonderful plush carpet before my house of swooping, leafy boughs. Beside those sunny clusters of purple sunshine winds a narrow path, slipping away to the heart of the woods. Nearby this lovely land is a towering oak, its base enshrouded with curious pieces and dainty violets, both purple and white alike. This realm of violets is the most wonderful place to relax.

-ARIANA MILLER (GRADE 8)

_____

_____

_____

_____

_____

_____

_____

_____

_____

_____

_____

STUDENT TIP:
This is a gold piece lesson. Restudy, edit, and revise your work. Refer to the rubric on the back page on the book for writing tips. Please write the final draft on the following blank page for your teacher to grade.

NAME _____   DATE _____

Read:

The boy, still half asleep, stumbled to his feet and, guided by the man's hand, fell into the seat. He began to eat the stew as if he were half starved, gulping it down like a hungry puppy.

The woman set a cup of milk before him, which he drank without taking a breath. "More!" he demanded.

"Hast thou no manners? A please and a thank-you come not amiss from children. Ah, especially for food such as this; the Prince himself of the highest seas has no better!"

The boy lay down his spoon frowning. "The Prince is not on the high seas. I am the Prince!"

Those at the table looked at him for a moment. Certainly the dust-stained boy they saw before them no more resembled the son of their King than would any other roadside lad. His skin was burnt fiery red by the sun and wind. His hair was matted by dirt and perspiration. His hands were rough and dirty and his clothes were made of rough homespun worn by all the countryside boys. His companion looked at him gravely, offering no word of explanation.

"Thou the Prince! Ha! Ha! Ha! I warrant thee, were the Prince in thy place he would the grace and manners to be courteous to a woman!"

"But I am the Prince! My father is the King!"

-TAKEN FROM *YOUNG PRINCE HUBERT.*
HOOVER DESIGN, 230 WOLF RUN ROAD, PATRIOT, OH 45658. USED BY PERMISSION.

Answer the following questions:

1. Could the boy possibly have truly been the Prince?

2. If he was the Prince, why wasn't he courteous?

3. Why do you think the boy was in this situation?

4. What are five ways to show courtesy to someone?

5. Why should ladies always be treated with respect?

NAME _____   DATE _____

Alliteration is the repetition of beginning sounds in words that are closely connected. Authors use alliteration to add sparkles to plain writing.

Overdone examples:

1. Alison aids Annie by aiming an apple at an alligator.

2. Simultaneously the seals sampled sneakers, salamanders, and smarties.

3. Rabbit Roy raced Rover right past rolling rattle snakes.

Regular example:

"They're – they're not – pretty," said Anne remorsefully.

"Pretty!" Marilla sniffed. "I didn't trouble my head about getting pretty dresses for you. I don't believe in pampering vanity, Anne. I'll tell you that right now! Those dresses are good, sensible, serviceable dresses, without any frills or furbelows about them, and they're all you get this summer. The white gingham and the blue print will do for you for school when you begin to go. The sateen is for church and Sunday School. I'll expect you to keep them neat and clean and not to tear them. I should think you'd be grateful to get most anything after those skimpy wincey things you've been wearing."

-EXCERPT FROM *ANNE OF GREEN GABLES*, CHAPTER 11

Your turn!

Write three overdone examples:

1. _____

   _____

2. _____

   _____

3. _____

   _____

Write a regular example...

...about your pet.

1. _____

_____

...about your school

2. _____

_____

...about your family

3. _____

_____

_____

_____

_____

_____

_____

_____

_____

_____

_____

_____

_____

_____

_____

_____

_____

_____

_____

_____

_____

_____

_____

_____

_____

_____

NAME _____   DATE _____

Write a persuasive paragraph with five supporting reasons. Brainstorm to come up with the ideas before you craft the paragraph. Remember to begin your paragraph with a topic sentence.

Options for other persuasive topics:

Why everyone should learn to swim

Why you should become a paramedic

Why you should learn another language

Why you shouldn't eat at McDonald's

Why you should be a business man instead of a missionary

Example paragraph:

I think that a farmer should raise beef cows instead of horses. First, beef cattle are something that man will always need to survive because they offer food substance. Man doesn't need a horse to live. Secondly, beef cattle need little care and looking after while horses need constant grooming and caring for. Thirdly, beef cattle don't need items like tack to be functional. Also, beef cattle are more docile and just plod along cow trails obedient-like while horses are high-strung and run away. Furthermore, beef cattle bring in more money than horses. Most importantly, I am scared of horses, so I'd much rather have beef cattle.

_____

_____

_____

_____

_____

_____

_____

_____

_____

_____

_____

_____

NAME _____   DATE _____

When you are having a terrible, horrible, no-good, very bad day, what normally happens? Tell us about it!

FREE WRITING PROMPT FROM THE BOOK TITLED *ALEXANDER AND THE TERRIBLE, HORRIBLE, NO-GOOD, VERY BAD DAY,* WRITTEN BY JUDITH VIORST

_____

_____

_____

_____

_____

_____

_____

_____

_____

_____

_____

_____

_____

_____

_____

_____

_____

_____

_____

_____

_____

_____

NAME _____   DATE _____

Make an acrostic by using the month that you are in right now. But this time, put the word at the end of the phrases. Describe your classroom, school, church, or recess activities.

Example: (describing the classroom themes):

Our door is graced with pine cone**S**

We are greeted with a welcom**E**

Before going into other classrooms we give their doors a ra**P**

If you go to the 3rd grade classroom you'll see an elephan**T**

Miss Steph's class is on an African adventur**E**

1st and 2nd grades work on a far**M**

Shhh! There shall not be in the halls any hubbu**B**

Did you know that Eeyore is her**E**

If you need a job go to the city of Webste**R**

_____

_____

_____

_____

_____

_____

_____

_____

_____

_____

_____

_____

_____

_____

_____

_____

_____

NAME _____   DATE _____

Read:

A Sample

I saw a tiny bite of moon,

All pointy at the edges.

It sailed upon a silver spoon

Through midnight's cloudy hedges.

I THINK I saw it softly stop-

(I did not have my glasses)

And catch a teensy, tiny drop

Of sparkling star-molasses.

Next night I went to look for it-

I wanted SO to taste it,

But the stars had licked up every bit-

I HOPE they did not waste it.

-SHEILA J. PETRE

Taken from FRESH AND FRUITFUL by Christine Laws.

Answer the following questions:

1. What did the poem make you want to do?

2. What shape would the "tiny bite of moon" refer to?

3. When is your favorite time to watch the moon?

4. Why do you think the author didn't want the stars to waste the star molasses? ☺

5. What was your favorite word picture in this poem?

NAME _____   DATE _____

Today, write a form of poetry called Haiku. Haiku is a Japanese form of poetry with seventeen syllables. However, when Haiku poems are translated into the English language, they no longer have seventeen syllables. The main idea of Haiku is to evoke mental pictures of anything having to do with nature using short, incomplete phrases. The poem doesn't have to rhyme.

Example:

Newly fallen snow

And glistening puddles of rain

Both reflect sunlight.

Darkness, at sunrise

Mysteriously recedes

Until the sun sets.

-MARY ELLEN MAST (GRADE 8)

Nature ideas to write your poem about:

Your mom's rose bush, an soaring eagle, whispering pine trees, swaying prairie grass, a gurgling creek, your pet horse, dazzling sunsets, etc.

Expand the lesson by inscribing your Haiku poems onto chalkboards or painting them on rocks, or using decoupage to glue them to flower pots.

You try it! ☺

_____

_____

_____

_____

_____

_____

_____

_____

STUDENT TIP:
This is a gold piece lesson. Restudy, edit, and revise your work. Refer to the rubric on the back page on the book for writing tips. Please write the final draft on the following blank page for your teacher to grade.

NAME _____   DATE _____

Since we're writing different styles of poetry, here is another one for you to try! You simply focus on a certain color throughout the whole poem.

Example:

Orange is Florida

It's laughing with friends

It's exciting and joyful

It makes you feel like cartwheeling.

Orange is the beach

Blue waves and palm trees

It's brown feet wearing flip-flops

Orange is running, running, running.

Orange is doing something new

Like riding a unicycle, snorkeling,

Or searching for a pirate's treasure.

Orange is full of life!

-ARIANA MILLER (GRADE 8)

Now, you pick a color and try it.

_____

_____

_____

_____

_____

_____

_____

_____

_____

_____

NAME _____   DATE _____

Just imagine what this world would be like if almost everything was made out of ice cream! Would it be cold in our houses? Would the ice cream clouds in the sky melt? What kind of ice cream would our cars be made of? Would there be flowers made of ice cream? Would the animals get frost bitten feet?

Describe what you think an ice cream world would be like.

_____

_____

_____

_____

_____

_____

_____

_____

_____

_____

_____

_____

_____

_____

_____

_____

_____

_____

_____

_____

_____

_____

NAME _____   DATE _____

Have you ever given a speech in front of your classmates before? Practice makes perfect! Today you are going to write out a speech word for word. The speech will be a one and a half minute speech. Your teacher will give you a specific topic to write about.

Here are two examples of speeches done by 7th graders:

If Jesus was living in America right now, and would own a truck, what truck do you think it would be? Here are your options: An old rusted out, beat up truck that hardly runs anymore . . . or a brand new truck with all the bells and whistles. I think neither!

I think that if Jesus would drive a truck it would probably be a quiet and simple one. It would probably be white and clean and probably not any bigger than He would need. He would probably drive speed limits and slower (unless in an emergency). He would most likely be a careful driver, not wild and reckless. What about road rage? What if someone cuts him off or turns out in front of Him? Would He shake his finger at them, or beep His horn at them? I can't imagine that, can you?

If the truck broke down, (which he could keep from happening if He wanted to), Jesus would, in my opinion, go to a mechanic He knows He can trust. When it comes time to pay I think he would do it cheerfully and maybe even pay extra. And maybe at lunch time He would go out with the mechanic to show His appreciation and satisfaction.

I think I would like to drive with Jesus, wouldn't you?

-BENJAMIN MILLER (GRADE 7)

Do you think that Cabela's or Dick's Sporting Goods is more fun to shop at? In my opinion, Cabela's is more fun to shop at in many different ways. Some things I especially like are (1) it has a huge gun and bow selection, (2) they have a nice big mountain with wild life on it, (3) they have a fun shooting gallery, and (4) some of them have a delicious food deli serving wild game. But there are some good things about Dick's Sporting Goods. For example, they have a nice softball selection that I really like. They also have a huge camping department.

I am going to ask you which store you think is more fun to shop at.

"Ryan, which store do you prefer shopping at?" He says Cabela's because it has better selections of different products.

I definitely would much rather shop at one of these two stores than at Spector's-a material store! ☺

-LEVI MILLER (GRADE 7)

_____

_____

_____

STUDENT TIP:
This is a gold piece lesson. Restudy, edit, and revise your work. Refer to the rubric on the back page on the book for writing tips. Please write the final draft on the following blank page for your teacher to grade.

NAME _____ DATE _____

Read:

Trees

I think that I shall never see
A poem lovely as a tree.

A tree whose hungry mouth is prest
Against the earth's sweet flowing breast.

A tree that looks at God all day,
And lifts her leafy arms to pray;

A tree that may in Summer wear
A nest of robins in her hair;

Upon whose bosom snow has lain;
Who intimately lives with rain.

Poems are made by fools like me,
But only God can make a tree.

-SERGEANT JOYCE KILMER

Answer the following questions about the personification (giving something human characteristics) **in this poem:**

1. What is the tree compared to?

2. List the different phrases in the poem that use personification.

3. Describe in a sentence how you feel about trees.

NAME _____ DATE _____

Describe one of your favorite Bible stories in sentences. Each sentence should start with the correct letter of the acrostic "story". Try to list the main happenings of the story so your audience can easily get the summary of the whole Bible story. At the end, write a summarizing sentence about your Bible story.

Example:

She touched Jesus' hem to be healed of her infirmity.

The crowd pressed close.

Ordinary, incredulous disciples thought Jesus asked a strange question.

Right away Jesus asked, "Who touched me?"

Yes, the lady confessed, it was me.

Summarizing sentence: My favorite Bible story is the one about the woman who touched the hem of Jesus' garment.

You do it!

S _____

T _____

O _____

R _____

Y _____

Summarizing sentence:

_____

_____

_____

_____

_____

NAME _____   DATE _____

Find five words in the dictionary that you don't know. Write them in the blanks below. Then exchange books with a friend. You will write pseudo definitions for each other's words. Exchange books again once you are done. Then write the real definitions below the "made up" definitions when you are done. ☺

1. _____
2. _____
3. _____
4. _____
5. _____

Definition #1

Pseudo _____

Real _____

Definition #2

Pseudo _____

Real _____

Definition #3

Pseudo _____

Real _____

Definition #4

Pseudo _____

Real _____

Definition #5

Pseudo _____

Real _____

_____

_____

_____

NAME _____   DATE _____

Options:

My worst fear is drowning...

My definition of relaxation is...

The summary of my favorite book is...

One person's trash is another person's treasure. Why is that so? Where do you find treasures?

_____

_____

_____

_____

_____

_____

_____

_____

_____

_____

_____

_____

_____

_____

_____

_____

_____

_____

_____

_____

_____

_____

_____

_____

_____

NAME _____ DATE _____

When you are writing short stories, practice eliminating passive verbs such as was and were. Remember to *show* instead of *tell*. Pick one of the following subjects from the Bible and write a three to four paragraph story using colorful verbs, concrete nouns, and fresh ways of wording things.

1. The dead god that fell down before a living God.

2. Absalom's hair trap

3. Solomon's disobedience with the Amalekites

4. Goliath's rival

5. Peter walking on the water

6. Jeremiah stuck in the cistern

7. Paul escaping in a basket

8. Mary anointing Jesus with rich perfume

9. The Egyptian plague of frogs

10. The lost coin

_____

_____

_____

_____

_____

_____

_____

_____

_____

_____

_____

_____

STUDENT TIP:
This is a gold piece lesson. Restudy, edit, and revise your work. Refer to the rubric on the back page on the book for writing tips. Please write the final draft on the following blank page for your teacher to grade.   115

NAME _____ DATE _____

Read:

"And he (Elisha) went up from thence unto Beth-el: and as he was going up by the way, there came forth little children out of the city, and mocked him, and said unto him, go up thou bald head; go up, thou bald head.

And he turned back, and looked on them, and cursed them in the name of the Lord. And there came forth two she-bears out of the wood, and tare forty and two children of them. And he went from thence to Mount Carmel, and from thence he returned to Samaria."

KINGS 2:23-25

Answer the following questions:

1. What is mockery?

2. How serious is mockery?

3. How should we treat the elderly?

4. How should we treat our peers?

5. How can mockery be avoided at school?

_____

_____

_____

_____

_____

_____

_____

_____

_____

_____

_____

_____

NAME _____ DATE _____

Make a list of some of your favorite people: your best friends, your parents, your aunt or uncle, somebody from church, a cousin, a teacher, a minister, a clerk at a store, etc.

1. _____

2. _____

3. _____

4. _____

5. _____

Pick one of these people and describe that person's physical qualities as well as his or her character qualities. Think about their facial expressions, their clothing, what this person likes doing, how the person reacts to surprises, and why you enjoy them. Use specific, captivating words. Experiment with using metaphors and similes in describing their physical qualities.

At the end of the paragraph, be sure to add why you like this person.

Example:

Mr. James was the most comical teacher I ever had. Mr. James is short with brown hair. He often wore his canvas shoes and what we called an old-fashioned sailor hat. He is always ready for a game of chess. His brain was like a chess board because he thought so much about it. You should see him teach a class. He was so bouncy and excited he would jump all over the place like Tigger. He is never like Eeyore. I can still hear him say, "If you want to, you don't have to, but if you don't want to, you have to." Mr. James loves music and singing. He was also a stamp collector, though he says, "I won't spend a hundred dollars on one stamp." Mr. James was a super friend and teacher.

-AARON MILLER & BEN MILLER (GRADE 6)

_____

_____

_____

_____

_____

_____

_____

_____

_____

NAME _____   DATE _____

Do you know how to write a recipe? ☺ Today, come up with a recipe for a really good time for a . . .

. . . good school day

. . . relaxing Saturday

. . . nice Sunday evening at home

. . . exciting road trip

. . . birthday party

. . . writing class

. . . show and tell presentation

. . . evening by the campfire

Example: Recipe for a fun picnic at the lake

You will need: 1 whole family, 1 watermelon, 15 hamburgers, wood for a fire, 1 plate of veggies, 1 pan of O.Henry Bars, 5 packs of sparklers, 1 gallon of lemonade, 1 bag of marshmallows, Frisbee, camp chairs, and sheet music.

Directions: Stick 1 whole family into van. Turn van repeatedly until it arrives at lake. Add wood to fire ring, light it, and begin to blow hard to start the fire. Layer hamburgers onto grate while children throw Frisbee back and forth quickly. Cut up watermelon and pour lemonade into cups. Lay out veggies and get O.Henry Bars ready to eat. Set around camp chairs. Enjoy hot food. After main course is eaten, settle into chairs till it gets dark. Use the sheet music to send harmony across the waves on lake. Keep fire going and add marshmallows to puff. Swing sparklers into the air for a beautiful scene. Repeat step one. Then turn van repeatedly till it arrives at home. Serves 1 whole family for 1 whole evening.

Very wonderful recipe!

_____

_____

_____

_____

_____

NAME _____   DATE _____

Do we understand everything in the world? Of course not! There are things far beyond our comprehension. Sometimes even the simplest things in life are hard to understand. Make a list of ten to twenty things you don't understand. They can be simple or profound.

Examples:

1. Why are most cows in children's stories given the name Buttercup or Daisy?

2. How do companies make vegetable oil?

3. How do they build skyscrapers?

4. I don't understand how cell phones receive texts.

5. I don't understand how people get bored.

6. Why do babies know how to smile before they know how to frown?

7. Why are garden tea stems square?

8. I don't understand how cd's play songs

9. Why do boys think diesel smoke is cool?

10. Why does the person who often knows the least speak the most?.

_____

_____

_____

_____

_____

_____

_____

_____

_____

_____

_____

_____

NAME _____   DATE _____

To "model" means to copy the pattern or replicate a product. Today, you are going to model a short poem. Read the following examples.

Examples:

A Fish	**A Rabbit**	**A Pencil**
A fish I considered myself	A rabbit I considered myself	A pencil I considered myself
But I hate the slime	But the lettuce I hate	But I abhor squeezing
And my breath I can't hold.	And the briars I fear.	And I can't stand up-side-down.
-JADEN YODER	-JONATHAN	-LORI MILLER

You try it! Pick three animals or inanimate objects and pattern your mini poems after these examples.

_____

_____

_____

_____

_____

_____

_____

_____

_____

_____

_____

_____

_____

_____

_____

_____

NAME _____   DATE _____

Read:

She did not know how long she slept. But she had been tired enough to sleep deeply and profoundly—too deeply and soundly to be disturbed by anything, even by the squeaks and scamperings of Melchisedec's entire family, if all his sons and daughters had chosen to come out of their hole to fight and tumble and play.

When she awakened it was rather suddenly, and she did not know that any particular thing had called her out of her sleep. The truth was, however, that it was a sound which had called her back – a real sound – the click of the skylight as it fell in closing after a lithe white figure which slipped through it and crouched down close by upon the slates of the roof – just near enough to see what happened in the attic, but not near enough to be seen.

At first she did not want to open her eyes. She felt too sleepy and – curiously enough – too warm and comfortable. She was so warm and comfortable, indeed, that she did not believe she was really awake. She never was as warm and cozy as this except in some lovely vision.

"What a nice dream!" she murmured. "I feel quite warm. I don't want to wake up."

. . . .

She knew it must be a dream, for if she were awake such things could not- could not be.

Do you wonder that she felt sure she had not come back to earth? This is what she saw. In the grate there was a glowing, blazing fire; on the hob was a little brass kettle hissing and boiling; spread upon the floor was a thick, warm crimson rug; before the fire a folding chair, unfolded, and with cushions on it; by the chair a small folding-table, covered with a white cloth, and upon it spread small covered dishes, a cup, a saucer, a teapot; on the bed were new warm coverings and a satin-covered down quilt; at the foot a curious, wadded silk robe, a pair of quilted slippers, and some books.

She sat up, resting on her elbow, and her breathing came short and fast.

"It does not melt away," she panted. "Oh I never had such a dream before."

. . . .

She sprang up, touched the table, the dishes, the rug; she went to the bed and touched the blankets. She took up the soft wadded dressing gown, and suddenly clutched it to her breast and held it to her cheek.

"It's warm. It's soft!" she almost sobbed. "It's real. It must be!"

She threw it over her shoulders, and put her feet into the slippers.

"They are real, too. It's all real!" she cried. "I am not, I am not dreaming!"

She almost staggered to the books and opened the one which lay on the top. Something was written on the fly-leaf, just a few words, and they were these:

"To the little girl in the attic. From a friend."

-EXCERPT FROM *A LITTLE PRINCESS* BY FRANCES HODGSON BURNETT"

Answer the following questions:

1. Who was Melchisedec?

2. Why was this girl sleeping in the attic?

3. Who do you think was this girl's friend?

4. Write two specific things you liked about the writing style of this excerpt.

5. Tell us about a dream that you have that you really wish would happen.

NAME _____   DATE _____

Write a three paragraph how-to article on one of the following ideas (or pass your own idea by the teacher)

1. How-to catch pigeons
2. How-to play soccer
3. How-to be a good hunter
4. How-to be a good dog trainer
5. How-to ride a horse
6. How-to be on time
7. How-to be yourself
8. How-to be creative
9. How-to get to know people
10. How-to learn to swim
11. How-to wash dishes
12. How-to throw a party
13. How-to clean out the barn
14. How-to drive a vehicle
15. How-to babysit siblings

HOW TO BE CREATIVE

1. spend time in nature
2. do things you're scared to
3. brainstorm alot
4. appreciate beauty
5. forget what others think

_____

_____

_____

_____

_____

_____

_____

_____

_____

_____

_____

STUDENT TIP:
This is a gold piece lesson. Restudy, edit, and revise your work. Refer to the rubric on the back page on the book for writing tips. Please write the final draft on the following blank page for your teacher to grade.

NAME _____   DATE _____

Scuttle, scuttle, little roach –
How you run when I approach:
Up above the pantry shelf,
Hastening to secrete yourself.

Most adventurous of vermin,
How I wish I could determine
How you spend your hours of ease,
Perhaps reclining on the cheese.

Cook has gone, and all is dark –
Then the kitchen is your park;
In the garbage heap that she leaves
Do you browse among the tea leaves?

How delightful to suspect
All the places you have trekked;
Does your long antenna whisk its
Gentle tip across the biscuits?

Do you linger, little soul,
Drowsing in our sugar bowl?
Or, abandonment most utter,
Shake a shimmy on the butter?

Do you chant your simple tunes
Swimming in the baby's prunes?
Then, when dawn comes, do you slink.
Homeward to the kitchen sink?

Timid roach, why be so shy?
We are brothers, thou and I.
In the midnight, like yourself,
I explore the pantry shelf.

-CHRISTOPHER MORLEY

Either write a story of a roach in the kitchen, or discuss who the "other being" as explained in the last stanza is, or draw pictures that go with every stanza (if your teacher allows you).

_____

_____

_____

_____

_____

_____

_____

_____

_____

_____

_____

_____

_____

_____

_____

_____

_____

_____

_____

_____

_____

_____

_____

_____

_____

_____

_____

_____

_____

NAME _____ DATE _____

I keep wondering if…

_____

_____

_____

_____

_____

_____

_____

Wouldn't it be fun if we could…

_____

_____

_____

_____

_____

_____

_____

_____

Hey, I have an idea! Let's…

_____

_____

_____

_____

_____

_____

_____

_____

NAME _____ DATE _____

Write a list of some of the things that people could possibly be doing around the world right now!

_____

_____

_____

_____

_____

_____

_____

_____

_____

_____

_____

Expand the lesson: Arrange the phrases into categorized, poem-like stanzas. It doesn't need to rhyme.

Example:

Sleeping, throwing pillows

Dreaming, waking early, snoozing

Carrying water from the well,

Petting monkeys, giving a safari tour

Flipping burgers, chopping lettuce

Giving a free soda away.

Camping, sky-diving, para-gliding,

Running races, swimming, boating...

_____

_____

_____

_____

NAME _____   DATE _____

Read:

"Sometime," said Phronsie, with her mouth half-full, when the meal was nearly over, "we're going to be awful rich; we are Ben, truly!"

"No?" said Ben, affecting the most hearty astonishment; "you don't say so, Chick."

"Yes," said Phronsie, shaking her yellow head very wisely at him, and diving down into her

cup of very weak milk and water to see if Polly had put any sugar in by mistake—a custom always expectantly observed. "Yes, we are really, Bensie, very dreadful rich!"

"I wish we could be rich now, then," said Ben, taking another generous slice of brown bread; "in time for mamsie's birthday," and he cast a sorrowful glance at Polly.

"I know," said Polly; O dear! If we only could celebrate it!"

"I don't want any other celebration," said Mrs. Pepper, beaming on them so that a little flash of sunshine seemed to hop right down on the table, "than to look around on you all; I'm rich now, and that's a fact!"

"Mamsie doesn't mind her five bothers," cried Polly, jumping up and running to hug her mother, thereby producing a like desire in all the others, who immediately left their seats and followed her example.

"Mother's rich enough," said Mrs. Pepper, her bright, black eyes glistening with delight, as the noisy troop filed back to their bread and potatoes; "if we can only keep together, dears, and grow up good, so that the Little Brown House won't be ashamed of us, that's all I ask."

-EXCERPT FROM FIVE LITTLE PEPPERS AND HOW THEY GREW BY MARGARET SIDNEY

Answer the following questions:

1. What makes somebody truly rich?

2. Why did Ben want to "get rich before Mamsies' birthday?"

3. What makes this family scene especially endearing?

4. Describe some riches your family possesses.

NAME _____   DATE _____

Find an object around the room or outside, like a clock, a book, a Rubik's cube, a backpack, a tree, a cloud, or something of that sort. Then write three four-lined riddles describing the item without saying what it is. Make the second and fourth line rhyme.

Example:

I'm gentle as a kitten

But I can conquer trees

And whip the waves in action

Across the stormy seas

Who am I?

-ARIANA MILLER (GRADE 8)

_____

_____

_____

_____

_____

_____

_____

_____

_____

_____

_____

_____

_____

_____

_____

_____

_____

NAME _____   DATE _____

Compliments! Have you given somebody a compliment today? Or maybe somebody gave you one. We all love a compliment now and then. Not a flattery, gushy type of compliment, but a down-to-earth sincere compliment. Today, write the name of each person in your classroom including the teacher. Then write one compliment for each person in your classroom including your teacher.

1. _____
2. _____
3. _____
4. _____
5. _____
6. _____
7. _____
8. _____
9. _____
10. _____
11. _____
12. _____
13. _____
14. _____
15. _____

_____
_____
_____
_____
_____
_____
_____
_____
_____
_____

NAME _____   DATE _____

Start With the Heart

I shrink to think

About the ink

That remains in my pen right now.

I strain my brain-

Alas, in vain!

I should write down my thoughts, but how?

Oh, wait! I'm late!

I missed my date-

I forgot the important part.

I pray and lay

Aside my way,

And I ask that God guide my heart.

-CHRISTINE LAWS

_____

_____

_____

_____

_____

_____

_____

_____

_____

_____

NAME _____   DATE _____

You've probably seen a grocery list before, but have you ever made one? Pretend you are planning for one of the following events, and then make a shopping list for that certain event.

Event ideas:

-Camping Friday night with school friends

-Father's day meal for Sunday dinner

-Picnic on the beach

-16th birthday party

-Spelling Bee

-Garden tea party

-Bike ride/hiking outing

-Teacher's supper

-Ice skating party

-Firewood splitting work bee snack

_____

_____

_____

_____

_____

_____

_____

_____

_____

_____

_____

_____

_____

_____

_____

_____

_____

NAME _____   DATE _____

Read:

"But now thus saith the Lord that created thee, O Jacob, and he that formed thee, O Israel, Fear not: for I have redeemed thee, I have called thee by thy name; thou art mine.

When thou passest through the waters, I will be with thee; and through the rivers, they shall not overflow thee: when thou walkest through the fire, thou shalt not be burned; neither shall the flame kindle upon thee.

For I am the Lord thy God the Holy One of Israel, thy Saviour: I gave Eygpt for a ransom, Ethiopia and Seba for thee.

Even every one that is called by my name: for I have created him for my glory, I have formed him; yea I have made him.

I am the Lord, your Holy One, the creator of Israel, your King."

-ISAIAH 43: 1,2,3,7,& 15

Answer the following questions:

1. If you could give a title to the following passage, what would it be?

2. Why are we created?

3. How do these verses make you feel?

_____
_____
_____
_____
_____
_____
_____
_____
_____
_____
_____

NAME _____ DATE _____

Write ten different things a person your age should do to have a good life. ☺

Examples:

1. Be courteous to others
2. Honor your father and mother
3. Drink lots of chocolate milk ☺
4. Read lots of books
5. Go on long bike rides with your friends

You do it!

1. _____
2. _____
3. _____
4. _____
5. _____
6. _____
7. _____
8. _____
9. _____
10. _____

_____

_____

_____

_____

_____

_____

_____

_____